Turtles

What Is a Turtle?	2
Where Do Turtles Live?	10
What Do Turtles Eat?	14

Written by Avelyn Davidson

What Is a Turtle?

A turtle is a reptile. Snakes, lizards, and crocodiles are all reptiles, too, so in some ways, they are alike.

Have you ever seen any reptiles?

A snake

A lizard

A crocodile

Did You Know?

We call reptiles "cold-blooded." Their body temperature changes with the temperature of the air or water around them.

He has been handling a turtle, so now he must wash his hands.

A turtle's shell is very hard.
Its beak is almost as hard as its shell.
A turtle has a tongue,
but it doesn't have teeth.
It has large eyes and it can see very well.
Its skin is like leather.

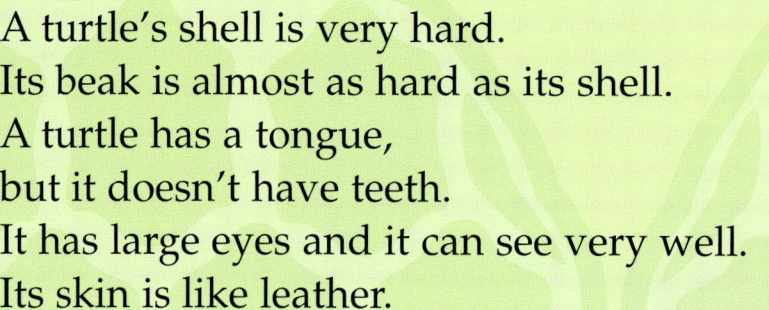

The turtle's shell

The turtle's tail

The feet

The beak

The mouth

The tongue

Did You Know?

A turtle can pull itself into its shell just like a snail. It protects itself that way.

The neck

The claws

A turtle has a pattern on its shell.
Its skin has a pattern, too.

The pattern on each turtle's shell is unique. It is different from any other turtle's pattern. The shell pattern on a turtle is like the fingerprints on a person. No two patterns are the same.

Turtles lay eggs. The eggs hatch,
and the baby turtles are born.
The babies have to take care of themselves.

A turtle lays her eggs

8

Did You Know?

Life can be dangerous for the turtle babies. Lots of bigger animals such as crocodiles eat them.

A baby turtle is hatching

A crocodile

Where Do Turtles Live?

Turtles live on every continent except Antarctica.
Turtles live in deserts, rain forests, and rivers.
They also live on mountains.
Some turtles live in ponds or streams,
and some live in the ocean.

Did You Know?

A tortoise is also a turtle.
A tortoise lives on land.

A tortoise

A turtle can stay underwater much longer than a person. But turtles still need to come up for air.

Did You Know?

A turtle can be a good pet.
Have you ever had
a pet turtle?
Would you like to have
a pet turtle?

What Do Turtles Eat?

Some turtles eat fruit, flowers, and leaves.
Others eat worms and insects.
Some turtles eat fish.
Have you ever watched a turtle eat?

Flowers

Leaves

Insects

Turtles can weigh as much as 680 kilograms

Index

babies	8–9
beak	4–5
cold-blooded	3
eggs	8
food	14
pets	13
reptiles	2–3
shell	4–7
skin	4, 6
tortoises	11
water	10, 12